HEARD

HOW LOSS LED US TO LOVE

HEARD

HOW LOSS LED US TO LOVE

ISBN 9781072859437

Library of Congress Control Number: 2019908579

Design: Heath Cushman
Photos: Marissa Lewis, Ligia Cushman

Printed in the United States of America

Visit my website www.ligiacushman.com

To Mami, the first person to tell me that I was born to write, when the world told me I was destined to fail. Te Amo Lela.

As a child, I struggled with many insecurities: I hated my unruly hair, had body image issues, and never felt pretty enough, but that all changed the first summer I spent with my cousin Ligia. As a child, she was the most confident, genuine and relatable person I knew. She was honest, direct and kind. I distinctly remember how much I admired her strong sense of self and the way she invested in everyone around her. She taught me self-love, she taught me the power of having positive self-esteem, and most importantly, she taught me self-worth. Michelle Obama once said, "Everyone just has to be themselves; if we are comfortable with who we are, that shines through." Discovering and shifting my perspective because of Ligia transformed my life, and I hope that her words will have the same effect on you. If you have ever felt unheard, let her story inspire you!

Dr. Clarybel Peguero
Senior Director for Volunteer Engagement
Duke University

CONTENTS

ACKNOWLEDGMENTS

No book is the product of the individual effort. This book is certainly no exception. Heard started out as a love letter to our son about our journey to him. Never in my wildest dreams did I think it would also be a journey back through some of the hardest times in our lives. Heard reflects the insight, creativity, editing and writing skills of a few talented folks I get to call family.

To begin, I'd like to thank our son Jaden for being the bravest kid I know. If it were not for his willingness to help those around him I would never be able to share this book with all of you. He believes adopted kids, like him, can change the world. This book is a small way to change the world.

On the creative content and production side of the equation, my husband, Heath Cushman, deserves far more credit than a sentence or two can provide. He is the genius behind the book cover, layout, and design. His insight on the design made this book visually a dream come true. I could have never done this on my own. 11:11

Many shout outs to Dos Cocos Locos Media Production for the amazing book promotion content. You made me look good even when I didn't feel good all of the time.

To L., thank you for your bravery. Your ability to plan for Jaden changed everything. Who knew a book would be born out of the toughest time of your life. May you always know that the weight and magnitude of your sacrifice are not lost on us.

To my siblings, your encouragement and support have meant the world to me. I know I am never alone because of the army I have surrounding me.

Most people have a tribe they can rely on. I am honored that my tribe of Jefas consist of amazing women who embraced the idea of the book long before I ever did. Thank you for your confidence and steadfast love. You all know who you are…Las Amo!

To Papi, thank you for teaching me to dream.

Books always reflect something of the author's story. This book is certainly no exception. May our story reach you and help you see that your darkest moments may be the exact path needed to step into your purpose. I know it was for me. So here we go…

FOREWORD

I distinctly remember the day Ligia told me she and Heath would be adopting a baby boy. At the time, she was an adoption social worker, and she told me of the first time she had met the birth mother. I remember Ligia sharing about their first encounter, when the birth mother saw a picture of her with her husband and realized they were interracial, she simply asked, "Would you want to adopt my baby?" A perfect match. What were the odds of this girl, needing a family for her unborn child, meeting Ligia at the precise moment that they wanted to grow their family through adoption? It seemed like destiny.

I also distinctly remember the pain and heartache—pregnancy, hope, miscarriage, loss—leading up to that day. I was young and newly married and didn't yet desire to have a baby of my own, so in many ways, I was merely an observer. I had no real understanding of the deep longing to become a mother, and what it would be like to have that dream ripped away, over and over. I was not yet aware of the toll it could take on one's body, mind and emotions. It would be years before I could even begin to understand.

A few months after that fateful conversation, we sat on a hospital bed, side-by-side, Jaden in my arms. Ligia looked over my shoulder, a radiant smile on her face. She was a mother. I was holding her baby boy. Her son. The one she had longed for, hoped for, prayed for. The one she had walked through the darkest season of her life for. What an honor it was to walk alongside her through that season, to have been a witness to the joy and the pain. Over the following months and years, we watched the Cushmans become a family. Hard, but happy days, sleepless nights, wondering and worrying if they were making the right decisions. New jobs, new homes, big moves. Life as a family, made possible through the gift of adoption. But also made possible through loss and pain and heartache. One didn't happen without the other. They are both a part of the story, hand-in-hand.

Ligia shares this story in a beautiful, honest and relatable way. I believe that anyone who has walked the road of infertility and loss will find great hope and comfort in the words in this book. Whether you are hoping to adopt, in the process, or just starting to consider it, this book is for you. This is Ligia's story, but it is also the story of thousands of other families. My wish for each of you is that through her story, you will find healing and hope.

Alison Little
Entrepreneur
Visual Uprising Photo

THOUGHTS FROM THE AUTHOR

Do you have a story? I'm pretty sure we all do. Does your story have value? Absolutely. Can your story influence others? Without a doubt. The Bible says we are chosen. So why is it that we are often reluctant to share the hard moments of our lives with others? I think sometimes it's because those hard times are reminders of the firm losses we have experienced in our lives. This story is one of tragic loss, grace, and love beyond all understanding.

I'm often asked why I finally decided to go live with my intimate life stories about loss, adoption, infertility, and our multiracial family experiences. It wasn't an easy decision. I am stepping into the purpose God has for me.

This book is about the hardest moments in our lives and the biggest lessons they have taught us. By no means is this book a how-to-parent-your adopted-child guide, because I fail at that all the time. This book is about one family's journey to adoption, how loss and love changed everything. It's the story of how God stepped into my mess and made it perfect in time. Our hope is that our story will help another couple or family step into their purpose of adoption.

Lovingly known as Moré (short for Morena, meaning pretty brown girl) by her family, Ligia was born in the Bronx to Dominican parents. When she was nine, her mom moved them to Washington Heights, a primarily Jewish and Dominican community. Her experiences in that community developed the foundation for who she is today.

Ligia shares that, "Growing up, I had to constantly justify how I was Dominicana. People had a difficult time with my complete package. My dark complexion and physical features didn't fit the traditional idea of what it means to be Latina. I am Afro-Latina and I love it. However, living in the hyphen of Afro-Latina is complex, beautiful, and at times bittersweet."

Ligia married her best friend, a white guy from Jersey, in 1999, and together they moved to the South. In the South, this love faced its fair share of challenges. In 2005, they adopted their then-infant son, who is multiracial. As an adoptive mom of a budding scientist, Ligia has had to face the hard truth that her son, with all his brilliance, diversity, and love of all people, will still face racial inequality in his lifetime.

With a master's degree in Professional Counseling and over eighteen years' experience as a social worker, Ligia oversees adoption services in Tampa, FL. Through her work, she finds herself educating and coaching others regularly on issues of diversity and culture. Her work has led her across the country, speaking on the needs of multiracial adoptive families and their related challenges. As a former college instructor, Ligia has challenged her college students to not judge a book by its cover but rather let a person's character help them see the true nature of that human.

As an influencer, writer, and speaker, Ligia shares many

personal experiences that provide teachable moments from her own life. Her hope is to raise awareness and change the narrative of what it means to be a multiracial adoptive family in a world that often wants to put you in a box. The belief that multiracial families can thrive is what drives her work.

1

THE LOSS

The clock's neon blue light flashed a glaring 3:23 a.m. In the stillness of the dark morning, my body betrayed me. The cramping was immediate and sharp. I woke up to it, bleeding, in a deathly silence that left me numb. Surrounded by the white cold walls, I quietly whispered, "God, please no."

Waking him, my best friend, up was the hardest part. A year of fertility treatments led us to the words we longed to hear: "You are pregnant." I didn't want to disappoint him. I knew he would never feel that way, but somehow if I woke him, the dream turned nightmare would be all

too real. But I gently woke him, and he rushed to my side.

The moments that followed are still hard to talk about. I anxiously waited for the ER doctor, whose name escapes me now, to tell me what I already knew. "Mr & Mrs. Cushman, you are experiencing a miscarriage. There is nothing we can do but wait it out."

Wait. It. Out. I remember thinking, What does that mean? Thinking about it and actually hearing it confirmed are two different things. Instantly, I knew my life was changed forever. You see, the fertility treatments had actually worked. I was pregnant for a little over twelve weeks when our baby went to heaven. The best part of the pregnancy was that I got to share it with my two besties who were also pregnant and due at around the same time. In my fantasy, we would raise our children together and complain about how we didn't know if we would survive the teen years. We didn't know much about our baby other than that the due date was set for November 26, 2005.

Returning home from the ER was hard. I was still "pregnant" and waiting for our baby to officially leave this earth. I decided then and there that I would never put my body or our marriage under such distress again. The risk was too high. That decision didn't make me any less angry. I was especially angry that God would allow me to endure such heartache. I was mad at everyone. What made this time even more difficult was that those two best friends were having completely healthy pregnancies. I was mad that God didn't hear me. He didn't hear my desire to be a mom. I was helpless.

To understand our journey to being heard, I invite you to our beginning. We were married in my home city, in a little red Spanish Baptist Church in Washington Heights, surrounded by two hundred friends and familia. It was a fairytale wedding with

ADOPTION ALWAYS STARTS WITH LOSS.

Cinderella ball gown and tiara to match. Our love was definitely (and still is) one for the books. Our marriage has taken me on some of the greatest adventures of my life.

Seven years later, we were finally pregnant and over the moon. One thing was true. Growing our family would not happen the traditional way. This was why the loss was hard on me. I felt robbed of the life we were trying to build. Many years later, my husband would say, "I was afraid I lost my wife in our loss."

My husband was my hero during this time. He didn't think much about himself. He only thought about me. Later, he would share that the hardest part for him was when I had to have a D&C.

Americanpregnancy.org describes the procedure as follows: A D&C, also known as dilation and curettage, is a surgical procedure often performed after a first-trimester miscarriage. In a D&C, dilation refers to opening the cervix; curettage refers to removing the contents of the uterus.

The contents, in my case, were our child. The loss of that moment will never be absent for us. I know I have a child who waits for me in heaven.

2

WHEN ADOPTION CALLS

What if God didn't meet your needs because He wanted to exceed them? He did that for me when He called our family to adoption.

I am a planner. A problem solver. That is why being a social worker for almost twenty years fits me. I love to help others achieve their dreams. This is why this season was so incredibly hard for me. There was nothing I could work on. Nothing I could fix. I had no influence or power. So when I brought my struggles to the Lord in prayer, I tended to also bring my carefully thought-out ideas and suggestions on how He could restore or change my situation. That didn't

"DO YOU WANT TO BE PREGNANT, OR DO YOU WANT BE A MOM? BECAUSE THE TWO ARE VERY DIFFERENT THINGS."

— Ligia Medina

work. That's when the words the doctor said to us echoed loudly in my head: *Wait it out.* It was in the waiting that my faith increased.

When May rolled around, I dreaded even the thought of Mother's Day. Those of us who are childless around Mother's Day know exactly the pain I speak of. As the world celebrates mothers, it feels as though childless women are forgotten. I was unheard and forgotten. It was definitely a painful time.

My husband was such a great support to me and did everything he could to bring me back. That Mother's Day was full of fun moments that had nothing to do with being parents, and I loved it.

I remember calling my mom and tearfully explaining why I would not be available to wish her a great day. I needed a break from the planning of a future that was not going to happen for me (or at least if felt that way at the time). As my good friends Madeline and Melissa planned beautiful baby showers, I quietly had to figure out how I was going to not attend. Living six hundred miles away made it easier. My grief was bitter and hard, and demanded that I be alone.

It is hard to wait on God when you want to move forward and you're seeking His guidance but He seems silent. I felt utterly alone trapped in God's silence. Have you ever blocked somebody's calls from your phone? I felt blocked by God.

You see, if He could keep me there in the space of loss, I could never step into the purpose I was originally designed to have. There was a purpose for our family through our loss. I simply didn't know it yet.

My mother and I have always been close. So when she said she was coming for a visit in August, I was excited. She, my stepdad, and Tia Irma hopped in the car for a sixteen-hour trip. If I am being honest, I longed for her company and my Tia Irma's arroz con gandules. What Mom shared with me during her visit changed my life forever. It was during that visit that God sealed our purpose as a family.

Sitting on the back deck of our small North Carolina home, my stepfather, in his brash way, said "What you need to do is adopt an orphan from the Dominican Republic." My family were immigrants from the Dominican Republic, so this logic made sense to him. I will forever love him for being the first one in my family to let me know that any child, adopted or not, would be cherished in our family. He's held tight to that promise.

What my stepfather didn't know is that Heath and I had already started the conversations about adoption. Mom would later share that she had been at a conference where she received a prophetic word that I was designed to adopt and would need to be obedient to that calling.

As I sat in the shock of what my stepdad had just boldly shared, Mom's next question was simply, "Do you want to be pregnant, or do you want to be a mom? Because the two are very different things."

I was a bit taken aback by her question. Here was my Hispanic mother of six children explaining to me that being pregnant is but a brief moment in motherhood and that raising a child is a life-long gift. I didn't have to answer her. She and I both knew that motherhood was my heart's desire.

What made this time extra special is that it was my job at that point to find homes for foster children who were on the waiting list. Soon, adoption would not just be something I did for a living, but rather would become something I would live, day in and day out.

Lysa TerKeurst is an amazing believer, an adoptive

mother and one of my favorite writers. She once wrote, "We don't have to know the plan to trust there is a plan. We don't have to feel good to trust there is good coming. We don't have to see evidence of changes to trust that it won't always be this hard."

I needed to trust that our decision was perfect for us. Adoption was what we were destined to do. Becoming a family first required obedience in adoption. I often wonder what would have happened if Heath and I had made the decision to try one more time. Where would our young man be today? Would he even know that he was deeply loved, not just by our family but by our creator?

As beautiful as it is, the story of us started with an unbearable loss. The loss of the unknown child, who we would never kiss, never hear their laughter when Daddy made one too many Daddy jokes. As the months lingered, well-meaning people tried to cheer me up with well-meaning but insensitive comments like, "Well, at least you can have another one" or "When are you going to try again?" Trying again was the scariest part for us. We had to make a decision. Would we continue to chase after the maybe of pregnancy, or would we pursue our purpose in adoption?

For many months, I'd been trained by exceptional adoption professionals on the need for adopted children to be validated, to have a sense of belonging, and to have birth-family connections.

Never in my wildest dreams did I envision living out the things I was asking families to do with their adopted child.

Adoption had already entered my life professionally. Having been an adoption social worker for a little over two years, I knew the legal ins and outs of the business. If I'm being honest, that made it easier for me. Reflecting back on it now, I believe God used that work experience to prepare us for the journey that we were about to embark on.

3

IT'S A DATE

Two weeks after Mom's visit, we met the woman who would change our lives forever. She was small in stature, with bright blue eyes, long eyelashes, and dark brown, curly hair. She was beautiful and she wanted us to be the parents for her unborn baby boy. Our encounter was awkward, if I'm being totally honest. Remember, adoption is not a natural process. But her smile lit up the room, and something deep inside told me we could trust her.

Family members asked me over and over again, "What was she like?" and "Will she turn and run?" The Bible talks about having a peace beyond all understanding, and

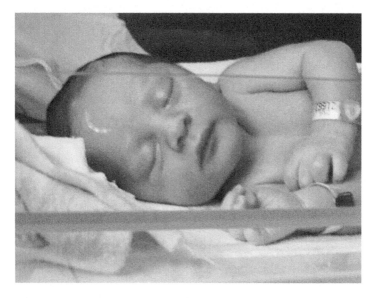

Just minutes after Jaden was born.

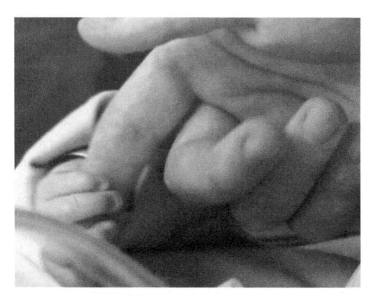

Just how tiny 5lbs. 15.5oz. is.

that is what I had during this process. The moment we met her, we were all in. She was not only beautiful on the outside—she had a caring heart. A heart that I would later learn our son would inherit (along with her curly eyelashes). Most importantly, she was committed to her decision. As time went on, we became friends, and later we would both become mothers. Can you imagine that? This stranger and I would share a son for the rest of our lives.

In the months leading up to his birth, we spent a great deal of time together. I accompanied her to medical appointments, chatted about her life over chicken nuggets, and discussed our hopes and dreams for Jaden. I knew she trusted us as well when she introduced the idea that I be in the delivery room with her. "It makes sense that you should cut the cord," she said. What sticks out to me the most was her desire to give our son (hers and mine) the life she never had.

Far too often, we think of the birth parents as bad people. We, the adoptive parents, believe we are the savior of the child we are adopting. In reality, it is our children who end up saving us. Our son has taught us of forgiveness and faith just by being born.

In hindsight, I can say that we grew to love her before we even met him. Loving her was something I could not have anticipated, and yet it was easy. You see, how could I not love the woman who gave me my son? Without her life and love, I would not be a mother, and the magnitude of her sacrifice is not lost on me.

The best part was that, as we started discussing it, she was seven-and-a-half months pregnant, which meant he was going to arrive sooner than later. As we met with the adoption attorney, I remember how her bright blue eyes filled with joy when we talked about the life our baby would live. The most unexpected Godly moment was when

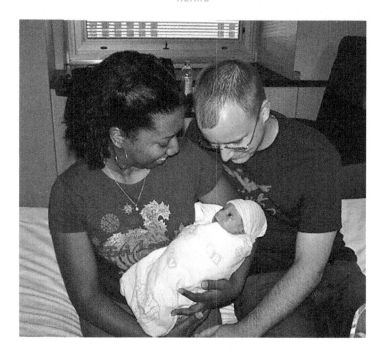

she told me her due date: November 26, 2005.

I couldn't catch my breath fast enough. She softly repeated it again. November 26, 2005. Here we were, about to watch our beautiful (adopted) son be born the same exact date that our child had been due. How could that be? Only God could make such a miracle.

This was the first of many times I felt heard by God during our journey. After that, when challenges in the adoption arose, I remembered that date and I was surrounded by peace. It was God's firm promise to our family.

Meeting her this far along in her process meant everything had to be expedited, from the home study to the baby shower. For those of us who know the risk in adoption, I was not comfortable with having a baby shower until after the days that the birth mother could legally relinquish him had passed. That meant we waited the eight long days to ensure we could keep him. I told my family and friends to refrain from sending gifts until we were out of the waiting period. But boy am I glad no one listened!

The gifts just kept coming. Remember those friends who were pregnant at the same time as I was? Based on their due dates, I would be the first to be a mother. Can you imagine that? Just a few short months prior, I thought all hope was lost. I felt lost, but God heard me in my despair.

A month and a half later, on a warm November morning, the phone rang. Her water had broken and the contractions were strong. He was coming. He was coming twenty days early. She wanted us to meet her at the hospital. My heart stopped. I looked at Heath and he was pale white (more so than usual!) We were both frightened young kids about to take a leap of faith into the unknown.

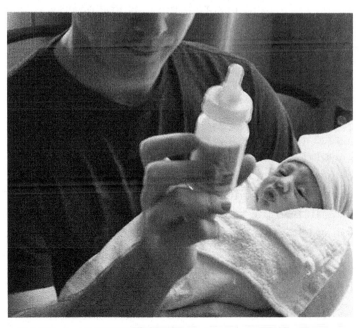

Everything moved very quickly after that. I remember getting in the car and thinking, *When we come back home, we will be parents.*

If I'm being honest, there was a fear that set in as well. What if after she met him she would decide not to place him with us? What if she couldn't do it after she actually saw her eyes staring back at her? What if all the promises of being heard were snuffed out in one moment? That's when I remember God gently reminding me that he was in control, no matter the outcome. He reminded me that He'd heard my prayers and knew what I needed. So, what else could I do but stand by my promise and step out in faith?

We arrived to the hospital with the car seat thrown in the back, the wrapping still on it. We went upstairs and spent an hour staring at one another, fueled with fear and anticipation. She was in pain from time to time, but you'd never have known it. This time reminded me that adoption, in all its beauty, is not a natural process. Every adoption experience is different, and I was standing in the middle of ours.

I sat with her, held her hand during the hard contractions, and quietly prayed for her and our son. After about two hours, as her contractions settled down, she encouraged us to go get some food in the cafeteria. I reluctantly agreed. I couldn't really eat, but I knew we had a long day ahead of us, and eating might fuel me for what would come. As we sat down to eat, the nurse called. "Get here now or you'll miss it."

I ran into the room and witnessed the moment my son entered this world. What an amazing, breathtaking moment God gave me. He was perfect. He looked just like her, but with bright hazel eyes. I cut the cord, while he sucked the doctor's thumb because he was ready to eat.

He was pink, perfect—he was our son.

The moments after our first meeting him, Heath, now and forever known as "Daddy," fed him for the first time. Actually, Heath was the first person on Earth to ever hold our son. How fitting. The person put on this Earth to be his protector held him close, providing for him moments after they met.

I believe becoming his father changed Heath forever. When evening set in, Heath went home to get the house ready for our guy before he came back. That gave his two moms some time alone.

Together, in that room with him, we both laughed, cried, and shared stories of our childhood. I tried to remember every detail of her story so that I could share it with him as he grew. This time together is forever etched in my soul. What I remember most of all is how peacefully he slept while we talked about him, and the hopes both his moms shared for him.

When the time came to go home, she left first. I can't imagine how hard it must have been for her to walk away. I went to say goodbye, embrace her, and thank her for her sacrifice and love. Adoption is hard. Its real people living through real loss. We both knew this would not be the last time we would see each other, for we were forever tied together.

I would learn later that a week after his birth, she reached out to our attorney—brokenhearted, depressed, and feeling betrayed by her body. What many people like me who have never given birth to a child don't realize is that while a woman is pregnant, her body is preparing to feed and care for an infant. Her breast milk continued to come with no baby there to nourish. This too would take time to accept.

4

WHAT'S IN A NAME?

Scripture tells the story of Moses, an adopted child, loved by two families. One family loved him from afar, while the other enjoyed his laughter and embraced his passions. The name Moses comes from the Hebrew word meaning "to pull out/draw out." You see, Moses was drawn from the water. In many ways, my Moses moment came when I cut the umbilical cord and saw our boy catch his first breath. Jaden was perfect in every way.

The next time I felt heard by God was at Jaden's third baby shower. Yes that's right he had THREE showers. It's funny, because we always tell others that our journey to

Jaden wasn't one that happened overnight. Heath and I waited seven years before we decided to grow our family. It wasn't always by choice. Heath will tell you I was ready to be a mom right after we got married. The reality is we weren't ready. God's timing was perfect.

For me, being a mom was also influenced by being the daughter of immigrants. My parents migration from the Dominican Republic to New York City in the late 1960s definitely shaped how I viewed family. Being raised in a

JADEN – *HEBREW, MEANING GOD HAS HEARD.*

home with six children definitely plays a role in how you plan to navigate your life. I knew that my parents' life map pushed me to be intentional about how I wanted to bring children into this world. Children I could teach not only about my faith but about this great big world that inspired me to serve others. Simply put, my parents taught me the value of children.

If you know anything about me, you know that waiting has never been easy for me. That's why waiting to grow our family was painful. There were many times my husband had to talk me off the proverbial ledge. Yet here were now were, beyond the wait.

When I think back on that time, I am reminded of Jacob, who waited for his wife for seven years. Of this time in Jacob's life, scripture says: "Jacob was in love with

Rachel and said, 'I'll work for you seven years in return for your younger daughter Rachel'...

So Jacob served seven years to get Rachel, but they seemed like only a few days to him because of his love for her." That last sentence really points to how I perceived that season of waiting. Today, that time of waiting for Jaden to join our family seems like only a few days because of our love for him.

When we were early in our marriage, we chose Jaden's name. We decided on Jaden Daniel. It was the name my husband, the artist, used as his pseudonym on all his artwork. At the time, we had no idea what his name meant. It wasn't until my friend Carrie, an amazing creative, decorated my baby shower room with the meaning of his name that I heard what Jaden actually meant.

We had many baby showers, and they were all after he was born. One was done in the home of our dear friends Alison and Scott. Another was held basically online by our entire family and friends across the country. Daily, five or six gifts poured in. Our biggest shower yet was at the Adoption Agency I worked at. It was beautifully decorated by Carrie, an amazing artist who could make any room look stunning. It was at this beautiful event that I was introduced for the first time to the meaning of Jaden's name.

There it was in black and white, laid out all over the cake table. "Jaden – Hebrew, meaning God has heard." Naming this book Heard was easy. God has heard every prayer I made for our son before and after his birth. This is the story of how God took our loss and led me to love in the most amazing way. He heard me and answered in a way I could have never imagined for myself.

5

THE LOSS AND GIFT OF HIM

Adoption is not natural. Anyone who tells you it is is lying. Adoption is about decisions. Decisions before, during and after the process. Adoption can be beautifully difficult. While we were on this wild ride to loving him and feeling heard in our journey, I cannot forget her. Her decisions started his journey to us. Her moment of feeling heard came by way of losing him. The weight of her decision is never lost on me.

In North Carolina, there is an eight-day waiting period where potential adoptive parents wait for the birth parents to essentially change their minds and ask that their baby

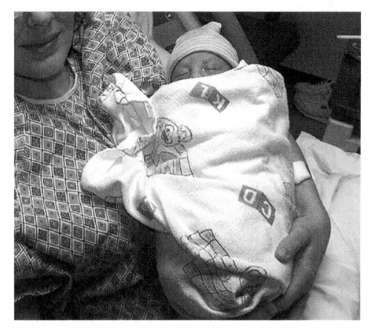

Jaden's birth mother carrying him the day he was born.

be returned to them. Although that waiting time was hard for us, we were distracted with baby rituals, feeding times, and transitioning to parenthood. She wasn't. Her hardest moments were ahead of her.

I often wondered about her. How hard/easy was it for her? What I knew was, shortly after walking out of the hospital, the magnitude of her decision hit her. She didn't regret her decision, but her body did. It demanded a child to feed and nurture. The breast milk didn't just go away.

There she was, waiting and ready to feed a baby. The pain of a breast filled with milk is uncomfortable for any breastfeeding mother. Many people don't think about what this does to a birth mother who has placed her child for adoption. You see for all the things we gained with Jaden, but she had real losses. Her breasts still wanted to feed a baby. Postpartum depression is a real thing. Can you imagine what postpartum looks like when you just placed your infant for adoption? I can't.

6

WHERE'D YOU GET THAT BABY?

Being heard in our desire to be parents couldn't have prepared us for what was to come. You see, bringing him home was the easy part.

I will never forget the day we brought our son home from the hospital. He was small, pink, and perfect. We were scared to death and overjoyed, all at the same time. I would imagine all first-time parents feel this way. I remember the first time I felt like we finally hit a routine. As many of you know, bringing an infant home from the hospital is no small task. I remember thinking, "Why did I move away from home again? Away from all my family

4 months old – first trip to NYC

and away from all the help in the world?" After weeks of no sleep and showering only when my husband got home from work, I finally felt like we had a routine. What our routine didn't include was a whole lot of outside time!

One particular afternoon, with stroller in hand, we braved the cold in the small town we lived in. We took a short tour of our local neighborhood, and at the end, when we had nearly reached our driveway, we saw our elderly neighbor from across the street come outside. She was saying something that I couldn't quite make out. I asked her to say it again as I hadn't heard her the first time. "Where'd you get that baby?" she repeated, this time a bit louder.

I could understand why she was curious. Having not been pregnant or discussed our adoption with anyone but close family and friends and seeing me here and now with this little baby must have been a shock. As our conversation continued, I quickly realized she wasn't curious but concerned. I graciously explained that we were in the process of adopting our handsome son, but her expression let me know she wasn't comfortable with the situation at all. What happened next still gives me chills. As I walked down the road, she

WHERE'D YOU GET THAT BABY?

called her nephew, a police officer, to come and figure out where I "got" our baby.

Think about that for a minute.

How did I feel when he approached me? How could I feel? Humiliated. Afraid. Here I was, with a government employee having to explain to another government employee who my son was and a brief story of his adoption. Humiliating for both him and me. I wasn't ready for that encounter, nor for many others we have experienced over the last thirteen years. I share most of these stories and what I have learned from them during my speaking engagements because I think it's necessary for other adoptive parents to hear that they're not alone and that they can thrive. The first lesson I immediately learned after this event was that this neighborhood would never fully embrace our family. That year, we sold the house and moved to a great neighborhood with very accepting neighbors.

"I was ill-prepared to address the interactions that were surely to come."

This encounter taught me that I was ill-prepared to address the interactions that were surely to come. Over the years, I have learned valuable lessons about how to parent in a way that embraces and educates our community regarding our multiracial family and our adoption journey. This is why I believe that parents who have adopted interracially need to understand that parenting your child will require additional skills that you may not currently possess, but that you can learn.

7

NOT UNICORNS

Oftentimes, people comment on how Jaden looks just like my family. He really does. However, adopting a child that "could pass as your own child" doesn't exempt you from racism. Becoming a multiracial family is something you expect when you marry interracially. Living in the South added its own special twist on the life we wanted to build for ourselves as a family. In a lot of ways, my family represents what I would call the "New South". We are growing our careers, buying homes and attending PTA meetings. We are doing life like everyone else.

However, adopting multiculturally required us to be

intentional about who we chose to navigate life with. Who were we inviting to our home? Our Sundays are spent at a multiracial church, where two of our core values are loving people unconditionally and standing united. On Sunday mornings, our Church truly contradicts Martin Luther King's thought that "the most segregated time in America is Sunday mornings." One of the things I love about living in the South is that there are certain pockets that are more diverse and progressive than many may think. That is why, as a born-and-bred New Yorker, I chose to stay.

However, we don't lose sight of the fact that it was just forty-eight years ago that our marriage was not only unheard of but forbidden in North Carolina. I often imagine what life would have been like for a child like Jaden (multiracial) born in a the 1960s. The amendment outlawing interracial marriage remained a part of the North Carolina Constitution until 1971. It still shocks me to know that less than fifty years ago, our family would not have been recognized as a family. I point all this out because this was the state where our son was born and raised for the first twelve years of his life. Today, while riding in the car after Scouts, Jaden asked, "Why did we move from North Carolina?" He's thirteen now, and it's important we inform him of the things he may not have noticed as a child.

My previous chapter, "Where'd You Get That Baby?" is a great example of how we experienced racism in real, tangible ways. I vividly remember the many times Heath and I would go out on date night (yes, after twenty years I still date my handsome fella), and we would be given separate checks. Small, I know, but it still has a huge impact. It doesn't happen every once in a while—it happens every time. If I'm being honest, that became harder to explain away as Jaden got older. I'll never forget the time my hubby went to a local pizza joint with our son and Heath was asked if he was our son's social worker. Or how about the time my son was called a "nigger" at summer camp by a four-year-old? I could go on and on about the disrespectful way some have treated our family, but when you are at the heart of changing the way people view families, it will come with challenges. I was naive to think that adopting a child that "could pass" as birth family would somehow protect him from the difficult moments we experienced.

It's not always easy to have to explain to our son at such a young age that some may never like him simply because he is multiracial. The first time we had to have this conversation with him was when he was just seven years old. That conversation was one of hardest I've ever had to navigate. Since then, too many times we have been forced to have difficult conversations with him about why things are different for us. So why stay?

WHY STAY...

We stay because we see hope. Hope in our friends who are raising multiracial children in our area. Hope in churches like ours showing what it means to love one another deeply. Hope in our family that we are changing the narrative about what it means to be a multiracial family in the South. Hope in knowing that our family is a Southern family with strong values and love of all people.

Seeing hope in our community carried us for a season. As he grew older, we knew challenges would come. Living in a small farming town in North Carolina didn't allow Jaden to be raised in a diverse community. The schools provided very little regarding diversity. I believe that this year was the first school year where Jaden actually had teachers who were African American and Latino.

Adopting interracially means that we need to make space for conversations about race with our child.

Although we knew we were part of the new South experience, we wanted a different version of the South that allowed us to see multiracial families in our community. Growing up in NYC, I took many things for granted, like having Jewish teachers who taught us about Hanukah or having friends who didn't look like me. In North Carolina, it was another story. Therefore, when I see others that look like us, I am excited. I want to run up to them and hug them. Don't worry, I don't. I don't stare or linger as many do when they see my little family, but it does warm my heart to know we are not alone in this world.

"IN NORTH CAROLINA, IT WAS ANOTHER STORY."

Seeing other multiracial families solidifies my thought that we are not unicorns. Now, don't get me wrong, I love Twilight Sparkle as much as the next guy! However, seeing other multiracial families in the South forces a new conversation. A new narrative, if you will. Our hardships have helped me prepare families for their multiracial adoptive experiences.

The new narrative is one that shows the world that multiracial families are strong and full of love. That we are thriving and happy and that it's ok to be different. It forces us to have tough conversations with our kids, so that they can have them with their friends too. We want a world in which multiracial marriages are not fetishized but rather welcomed into the fold. Staring at us while we are eating dinner or shopping at Target only makes someone look ignorant and makes our family feel isolated. We are not mystical beings; we are flesh and bone, just like you.

"UNICORN: A MYTHICAL ANIMAL TYPICALLY REPRESENTED AS A HORSE WITH A SINGLE STRAIGHT HORN PROJECTING FROM ITS FOREHEAD."

— Webster's Dictionary

I want people to know that yes, I am Afro-Latina, my husband is White, and we did raise our multiracial (adopted) son in a small farming town in North Carolina with the same hopes and dreams that they have for their families. Like many families in America, we want our son to grow up with a strong sense of family and hope that our relationship provides him with a model for what a healthy, loving partnership looks like. Like any family, we celebrate the ups and work through the downs together. Like all families in America, we are not unicorns.

STRIDING FOR OUR SON

Being multiracial in a small town was hard. As our son has grown older, we've found that living in an area that is demographically lacking in diversity is not the best for him. When you have a family that looks the same, you don't have to constantly justify that you are a family. I wrote about this in my blog post entitled, "The New South," where I talk a great deal about some of the toughest moments we have experienced as a family here in North Carolina. Moments like my husband being confused as our son's case worker rather than his daddy. Or times when my husband and I have had to navigate tough conversations with our son about being called the N-word, police brutality, and why people stare at us.

Over the last three years, my hubby and I have engaged in deep conversations about our desire for our son to experience many different people from all around the world. That is why we have traveled to many countries and cities with our little guy. In his young life, he has already traveled to New York City, Jamaica, the Caribbean, the Bahamas and Mexico, to name a few. We wanted him to know the world is big and full of different kinds of people. What we eventually realized is that we want him to have this rich diversity, not just on vacation but in his home community as well. For us to give him that, we knew that it meant we needed to relocate.

Often times, when I have led workshops for adoptive parents on embracing diversity and being intentional about the hard conversations surrounding race and ethnicity, they've asked me, "Should we move?" I will never forget the parent who emailed me after reading my blog and expressed that her soon-to-be adoptive daughter would "never be allowed to date outside of their race" because it "went against the Bible" (it doesn't). The hard part is that these adopted children didn't live in a community where they went to school with children who looked like them, and the parents had no plans to invest in building those relationships that would help their children navigate the world as children of color. It's moments like these that I think back on when I present at conferences, encouraging families to think differently and embrace change. Does that mean that every adoptive family should move away from their community to make sure their children get what they need? No. When I was interviewed on the Multiracial Family Man Podcast, I shared that loving an adoptive multiracial child is a beautiful thing, but that loving my son is not enough. Often times, love requires action. Action for another family may mean going to an African American barber in a different part of town. For our family, our action is striding into a new community, job and church. There were many reasons why relocation was best for us, and following are some of the most important.

STRIDING FOR OUR MARRIAGE

I'd like to think that anyone who spends time with us knows that we love each other deeply. It's hard when some in your community don't embrace that love. We knew, when we got married, that we would face adversity. I would argue the many multiracial relationships do. Being a multiracial couple has its challenges. The part of the country you live in can influence that greatly. We have lived in about five states. Some of the communities we've lived in made assumptions that we weren't together. We are typically offered separate checks at dinner and struggle with the million stares we get when we are out around town. I'm not saying the relocation fixed all the experiences we have had as a couple, but having less of it would be amazing. After relocation, I can honestly say that we have had beautiful moments. Most importantly, we are seen as husband and wife wherever we go. Many have embraced us, and I am happy to report that we see families that look like us all around us. The bottom line is that we want to live in spaces that make us feel less like unicorns and more like a loving couple. We are also keenly aware that in order for the South to change, families like ours need to be visible within the community. This is why we aren't leaving the South.

8

LIVING OPENNESS IN ADOPTION

When we finally decided we were going to move, I went on a mission to ensure our son got to spend time with those that mattered to him most. We knew that saying goodbye to his friends, family, and even teachers would be hard, but how do you prepare your child to say goodbye to his parent of origin? Adoption is real.

It's hard and it's beautiful. If you think about it, adopted kids have been saying goodbye to loved ones since before they could remember. At least for our little man, it was like this from the moment he caught his first breath.

This month, I had the honor of hearing April Dinwoodie,

adult adoptee and advocate, speak to a room of adoption professionals about the need for openness in adoption. April encouraged recognition that adoption is a human rights issue and not a one-time transaction. She described adoption as a lifelong journey. April boldly shared that children are not commodities. This phrasing brought it all home for me. I remember thinking, *He's not just our family.*

April noted that best-practice recommendations support children's basic human right to connect with and have information about their biological roots. This is why we have been so intentional to ensure that our son has information about his family of origin. However, having information was not enough—he needed connection as well. This is where adoptive parents can put their love in action. If it is safe, I am a firm believer that connection with biological family is critical to adopted children.

As we stride into the next chapter for our family, it means saying goodbye to loved ones. When you have an adopted child, it may mean saying goodbye to a biological parent they barely know. It may be awkward, but it's so necessary. So we planned a last Sunday for him to spent time with her. The woman who carried him has his same eyes.

He hugged her tight and held her hand. He asked me to take pictures. We took lots of them. He got to play with his baby cousin and meet his uncle and aunt for the very first time. We realized, in that instant, the magnitude of this moment. His two families sharing a time with him.

This visit was different from all the rest, because for the first time he met his extended family. It was magical. He played and laughed with them, gave hugs, and even asked to visit again before we took off to our new life and home.

I have discussed with him that moving away doesn't make her any less his family. People often ask us how we

_____

"FAMILY IS OUR CENTER OF GRAVITY."

_____

— April Dinwoodie

do it. How are we ok with having him spend time with her? As if love or the concept of family is confined to just us. We like to think of it as there being enough love for all of us. Our conversation with her is about a promise we made to her over twelve years ago. It was a promise to give him a full, happy life, and now this move is part of that promise.

Jaden hugging his birth mother before our move.

CHANGES IN COMMUNICATION

This isn't the end. It's the beginning of a new way to stay in contact. How will we modify our communication? We have decided to set up a private Facebook page for both families to connect and exchange photos. In addition, we will be intentional about visiting often. I hope our little man learns that in his life, he will sometimes have to say goodbye to people he loves deeply, but although those goodbyes will be painful, it doesn't mean those relationships aren't worth the pain.

As adoptive parents, we owe it to our children to find ways to honor their birth parents and families of origin. Connection is a way to honor their relationships.

9

ADOPTION AND THE CLASSROOM

Every year growing up, Jaden went to the same school with the same kids in the same community. Until now, he has been educated in a community that knew he was adopted. My striding brought him here. To this new space where his story would go from public to private until such a time that he felt comfortable to share. When he was nine years old, he stood before his class and shared his adoption story. I'm remembering his recollection of that moment, and he mentioned that the entire classroom gasped. The kids didn't know. The teachers did. That's why, when relocating, the mister and I did lots of research and chose the school before selecting our new home. We knew a good school was the key to his success.

When we first visited the new school, we let him set the pace and take the lead. He shook hands, introduced himself, and let people know what he needed. When it was all said and done, he said, "This new school is awesome!" For any parent who's relocated with school-aged children, you know it was a great relief to us to hear him say that.

One thing we didn't do was discuss the fact that he's adopted with his new school administrators. Why would we need to share that at all? Being an adoptive family adds an additional lens to every aspect of our lives, especially as it relates to school. I think we didn't touch on adoption on our first visit because, as he grows, we are encouraging him to set the pace on what part of his narrative he shares with the world. It's important that he knows he's adopted and that he decides who gets to know his story. Many adoptive parents don't always understand that our children have the right to say who gets to know their story and who doesn't. Even writing this book required Jaden's permission.

"I THINK TEACHERS SHOULD ALWAYS KNOW I WAS ADOPTED AND I WILL LET THE KIDS KNOW ONCE I CAN TRUST THEM."

— Jaden Cushman

The adoption process itself is in part to blame. When you are adopting, a big part of that journey is making it public. For those who require monetary support, sharing your story is a major part of that journey. A former adoption co-worker shared a story of meeting a dear friend's newly adopted daughter. After saying how cute the baby was, she bravely asked: "So, what's her story?"

What the adoptive mother said next changed our adoption journey forever. She kindly responded with, "we are not comfortable with sharing her story with everyone when she doesn't even know it. We'd prefer to keep it private for now." I thought their stance was impressive. From that moment on, both Heath and I agreed that we needed to set firm boundaries on how we shared Jaden's narrative.

"YOUR SECRET IS SAFE WITH ME."

When Jaden was younger, Heath and I navigated his story. Living in a small, rural community at the time, it was important for us to set firm boundaries as to who knew the details of his story and who didn't. Now that he's older and understands the concept of adoption, he gets to determine who knows and who doesn't. Because we made it safe to talk about adoption whenever he wanted, he now shares the fact that he is adopted with the world! Remember that first meeting with the new school? A couple of weeks later, at a parent meeting, Jaden shared that he was adopted with one of his teachers. She quickly replied with, "Your secret is safe with me." He quickly corrected that his adoption isn't a secret. I loved that! Our guy is learning to navigate a world that has its own thoughts about what a modern adoption should look like.

EDUCATORS & ADOPTION

With that said, I do believe that it is important, if not critical, that teachers know if they have an adopted child in their classroom. In my professional and personal experience, some adoptive parents don't always get why sharing that information is important. For our family, sharing that our child is adopted is very different than sharing his adoption story.

I have found that in today's modern adoption world, there are many tools for parents and teachers to use that help with engaging in an honest conversation about adoption. My good friends at the Quality Improvement Center for Adoption & Guardianship Support and Preservation developed an easy-to-read handout entitled "What Teachers Should Know About Adoption." As with any tool, take from it what applies to your family and chuck the rest. Another tool that has been invaluable for our family is the WISEUP workbook by the Center for Adoption Support and Education. This tool helps adopted youth and their parents roleplay how they would respond to tough questions about their adoption with peers.

Last night, I was discussing with Jaden how he felt about his sharing his adoption story at school. How he responded was pretty mature, if you ask me. He said, "I think teachers should always know I was adopted, and I will let the kids know once I can trust them." Here are three reasons we share that our son is adopted with his teachers:

ADOPTION-SENSITIVE CLASSROOMS

We want teachers to create adoption-sensitive classrooms. According to The Quality Assurance Improvement Center for Adoption and Guardianship, It's crucial that teachers know that some adopted kids are "grappling with issues related to identity, belonging, or attachment; managing complex and/or non-traditional relationships and roles with their birth family; experiencing loss and grief; and figuring out how to be in a family of a different culture or ethnic group."

ASSIGNMENTS MATTER

We desire a classroom that considers adopted children when selecting assignments and celebrating holidays. Often, family-tree assignments are difficult for kids who have been adopted. I do believe that assignments like these can help foster an intentional conversation with your child about adoption; however, it must be one that parents are aware of in advance. In addition, teachers may be open to modifying their teaching plans to be adoption-informed.

ADOPTION STATUS

We want to encourage teachers to recognize that children might be sensitive about their adoption status. It will help teachers be aware of conversations that may come up in the classroom. For some children, difficult anniversaries impact their ability to learn. Teachers who are aware of this can be a help to their adopted student rather than a hindrance.

According to the Institute for Family Studies, "Adoptive parents reported that an 83% majority of their children enjoyed going to school and nearly half—49%—were doing 'excellent' or 'above average' school work." With the right support and information, educators can help their adoptive students thrive.

Providing educators with information about our child's specific needs helps our son continue to learn and embrace his story. We believe our adoption story can be private, but it should never be a secret.

Every (new) adoptive parent should be prepared to navigate school systems. Remember that you are your child's advocate, and only you can bring your child's voice into a situation at school until they can do it for themselves.

10

CELEBRATE ADOPTION

Words matter. I think they matter even more if you have experienced adoption. Phrases like "your real mom" or "your real child" are difficult to hear and yes-adopted families hear these often. For example, the phrase "Gotcha Day" has sparked a huge debate in the adoption community.

WHAT IS GOTCHA DAY?

"Gotcha Day" is a phrase that denotes the anniversary of the day on which a new member joins a family through adoption. It is sometimes also called " Homecoming

Day", "Family Day", or "Adoption Day" – For many inter-country adoptive families, this day may differ from the actual adoption day. 'Gotcha Day' is often associated with annual rituals or celebrations.

Over that last few years, there has been a huge debate in the adoption community on whether we, adoptive parents, should celebrate our child's adoption day. Karen Moline, author and the adoptive mother of a child born in Vietnam wrote "Get Rid of 'Gotcha'" for Adoptive Families magazine in which she says: "Gotcha is my typical response when I've squashed a bug, caught a ball just before it would have rolled under the sofa, or managed to reach a roll of toilet paper on the top shelf at the store. It's a silly, slangy word...I find the use of 'gotcha' to describe the act of adoption both astonishing and offensive."

OUR DECISION

I have said it once; I'll say it again. Every adoption journey starts with a story of loss. This loss cannot be ignored or loved away. This loss can be ambiguous for the adoptee especially if they were adopted as an infant. So here is the thing most people may miss about adoption. Adoption is not just a story of loss. It starts there but can grow and evolve into so much more. To our family adoption is both an act of love and loss.

In our home, we use "Adoption Day" as a day to honor our story. Our story is hard, full of loss and surprisingly beautiful. However, many believe that no matter what name you use, Gotcha Day, Adoption Day, or Family Day it is a disingenuous day created by adoptive parents to celebrate their happiness while also possibly recognizing their child's loss. Some have even said that gotcha day is a narcissistic response to adoption by the adoptive parent.

It's tradition to celebrate his adoption day every year. As usual, it was low-key, quiet, and a private affair. As he has gotten older, he decides how he wants to spend this day and he always chooses to spend it with his family.

Never in my wildest dreams did I think that the child I prayed for and eventually adopted would think that my honoring his joining of our family, all be it an unnatural process, would be a way for me to boast about his loss. Those who know our story and our love for our son know we would never do anything to hurt him intentionally.

Articles like The Insensitivity of Adoption Day Celebrations by Mirah Riben, by the *Huffington Post*, challenged me. I began to think are my husband and I getting this all wrong? I decided to really go to the true expert. I took time to interview Jaden to learn how he felt about adoption and celebrating it.

Jaden calls his day "Adoption Day." Many of you have read about our mini superhero on my blog. He has been featured in posts like "Adoption: A glimpse into the day our son was born" and "Where did you get that baby?" which paint a picture of some of the beautifully complex moments adoption has thrown at us. His heart for people is evident in the way he loves his family. His insight on his own adoption experience is what has led me to share our story. Jaden will be the first to tell you that when it comes to his adoption he has double-dipped feelings about it. Double dipped is a terminology I taught him early on to help him understand that you could feel happy and sad about a thing and that is totally ok. As he has grown he's embraced quite adoption celebrations and big large ones too.

Jaden will be the first to tell you that adoption does start with loss, but it doesn't have to end there. Over time it can become many layers to a complex journey. It's important that we as adoptive parents not only celebrate our child's journey into our family but also that we honor their story before us. No matter what word you choose to celebrate your child's day, the important thing is to celebrate your child.

11

LOVE IS NOT ALL YOU NEED

The month of November is forever etched in my heart. It's the month when we are intentional about giving thanks. It's when we celebrate Adoption Awareness Month across the nation, but most importantly, it's the month we were heard and started our journey to parenthood.

I wasn't supposed to be a mom. At least, not the traditional way. That night our baby died is forever etched in my soul. Yet God blessed me with a wonderful opportunity to see our son be born. The moment he caught his first breath, my heart was forever changed.

As he has grown older, his understanding of adoption

"MOMMY, WERE MY **REAL** PARENTS MARRIED?"

has grown as well. Recently, I asked Jaden a series of questions about his adoption experience. Here are some (not all) of his thoughts about his adoption story.

"Adoption makes me both happy and sad. I love my life with you and Daddy and at the same time I miss them [my first family]."

This is what I call double-dipped feelings. Double-dipped is when an experience gives you happy and sad feelings at the same time. That's really how adoption feels for many adopted youth.

As adoptive parents, we have an opportunity here to have honest dialogue with our children about the complexities that come with adoption and that it's ok to have both sets of feelings. It's natural to feel this way. We should never take offense to it or expect them to be thankful for being adopted.

When I asked my son if love was enough in adoption, he surprised me when he said, "Love is enough because without you and Daddy loving me, even when I mess up, my life would be a sad place. It's enough because you guys do so much for me. You buy me stuff"—(he's rotten and it's all my fault)—"you teach me to be kind and we talk about adoption whenever I want to."

I'd like to focus on his last point. *We encourage him to talk about adoption whenever he wants.* As an adoptive parent and professional, I believe love can be enough when followed by action.

In my interview on the Multiracial Family Man Podcast, with Alex Barnett, he asked me my thoughts on what love needs to look like for an adopted child. In that interview, I said, "Love must be followed with action." However, action requires honesty, commitment and flexibility, and places our son at the center, not us. Love brought us to him, and action in love keeps us growing together. This means that fostering a relationship with his first family is our obligation as his parents. We don't wait for him to bring up his birth mom. We do it. We make it a safe space to talk about his real feelings.

SHOULD ALL KIDS KNOW THEY ARE ADOPTED?

Often, I am surprised when a family reaches out for my advice on when is the right time to tell their child they are adopted. My answer is always the same: "Yesterday." I asked

Jaden the same question, and his response was, "Wait, some kids don't know they are adopted? Why not? Yes they should know! It's their story and their right to know. Right, Mom? I'm so glad I know, even when it makes me sad sometimes."

Some adopted families are unique in that we are the keepers of our child's story. We dictate when and how we share it. It requires having difficult conversations when you least expect it, like the time he was a ring bearer at my sister's wedding and right after he exited the sanctuary and we were ready to take photos, he tugged my dress and asked, "Mommy, were my **real** parents married?" Or how about the time we had the sex talk but couldn't do that without him asking questions about when his birth mom became pregnant with him.

As adoptive parents, we never know what moment will prompt a conversation about adoption. What I do know is that, just like when he asked the question at my sister's wedding, I dropped everything, took him to the side ,and answered his question. We have to make time for the tough conversations, even in the most inopportune moments.

When Jaden was asked what he would like his family to know about his feelings surrounding adoption, he said, "I have a big family, from my birth parents (my first family) to yours and Daddy's family. I think of myself as the cornerstone. I connect all of you." Webster defines the word "cornerstone" as, "an important stone that forms the base of a corner of a building, joining two walls." He is what joins us.

How incredible is this child of mine? His ideas of love and adoption go hand in hand. Isn't that what the Lord wants to teach us about how He loved us?

Our son was born knowing what it means to have loss and love. We have always told him how happy we are that he was adopted, and at the same time we understand that those feelings of joy are tied to loss for him.

Our son loves hard. He adores his grandparents and misses his cousins when they are gone. His uncle Alex is the coolest guy he knows, and he knows his aunties, even his Titi Yvette, will buy him whatever he wants.

A great example of this is our recent family (indoor) sky-diving trip. He wanted everyone there (cousin's, titi, etc.). Our love for him is mutual, so that meant that although we were freaking out, we would all be there. You see, even though we were all terrified and he was straight up fearless, he taught us a valuable lesson. Often, adoption may feel like free falling. There's no real clear direction. But in the end, with the right support, love, and commitment, you can soar high!

Every day, this child, this young man, teaches us what it means to be an amazing human being, to love well and be exactly who God created us to be. That is how adoption has changed my life forever. It continues to teach me that love may not be enough, but it is an amazing place to start.

12

HEARD

I recently came across an amazing blog on adoption and foster care by Jason Johnson. In it, he states, "The gospel of our adoption, making its vivid debut that night in Bethlehem, acts not only as the emphasis behind why; but also the model of how we as those adopted into the forever family of God are called to forever give our families to those who need them."

That last line broke me. If I'm being honest, I have always felt that his adoption was a selfish move on our part because of our infertility. We wanted to grow our family, and this was the way we could do it. Over the years, that

THERE'S NO TELLING WHERE OUR ADOPTION JOURNEY WILL TAKE US FROM HERE,

BUT I KNOW IT WILL BE A PLACE WHERE OUR STORY WILL HELP OTHER COUPLES FEEL HEARD.

idea has evolved. I never truly understood the magnitude of what we were doing for our child. Once I understood it, I came to understand God's love for me. We are not the heroes in this story, Jesus is the hero of this story. We are not the heroes in our son's story. Jesus is.

God didn't meet my expectations, because he wanted to exceed them.

The pain and loss we experienced in March of 2005 was unbearable and, in many ways, unforgettable. When you lose a child through miscarriage, it's tough, and it's really about grieving the unknown.

Six months later, our lives were radically changed when I witnessed the birth of our son. I love him deeply. Nothing he does can ever change that. He is ours, and we are forever in love with the magic that is Jaden. He has taught me the true meaning of what it means to be loved by our savior.

Our adoption story started with loss, which led us to love. If it were not for that loss, I would not be speaking about our journey to adoption at national conferences. I would not be the Director of Adoptions at a child welfare agency, where I get to serve pre-adoptive and adoptive families, helping them in the way I would like to be treated. There's no telling where our adoption journey will take us from here, but I know it will be a place where our story will help other couples feel heard.

In his book, *MiCasa Uptown*, my dear friend Rich Perez shares that the "goal is to change well, to grown in love; the journey, in large part, is about learning to experience a radical, dynamic, yet uncompromising love that accepts you as you are but could never leave you as you are." Our journey to love has changed us forever. I simply don't remember life before Jaden.

Adoption does start with loss, but it doesn't have to end there. Over time, it can become many layers to a complex journey. It's important that we as adoptive parents not only celebrate our child's journey into our family, but also that we honor their story. No matter what word you choose to celebrate your child's day, the important thing is to celebrate your child.

ABOUT THE TYPE

The body text is set in Adobe Caslon Pro. For her Caslon revival, designer Carol Twombly studied specimen pages printed by William Caslon between 1734 and 1770. Adobe Caslon Pro is the right choice for magazines, journals, book publishing, and corporate communications.

Bison is a strong fontfamily and sophisticated sans serif created by Ellen Luff. Inspired by the animal, it's sturdy uncompromising style is felt through the controlled letterforms and modern touches. A balance of hard lines and smooth curves. Each font in the family can stand on its own, dynamic and authoritative in their own right. Bison was used for the title, headers and subheaders throughout.

NOTES

CHAPTER 1. THE LOSS

1. Cinderella. Dir. Clyde Geronimi, Wilfred Jackson, and Hamilton Luske. Perf. Ilene Woods. Disney, 1950. DVD.
2. D&C Procedure After a Miscarriage: Risks & Complications. American Pregnancy Association. July 18, 2017. Accessed March 18, 2019. https://americanpregnancy. org/pregnancy-complications/d-and-c-procedure-after-miscarriage/.

CHAPTER 2. WHEN ADOPTION CALLS

1. Terkeurst, Lysa. "What Ignoring God Could Have Cost Me." Lysa TerKeurst. April 2015. Accessed June 03, 2019. https://lysaterkeurst.com/2015/04/what-ignoring-god-could-have-cost-me/.

CHAPTER 4. WHAT'S IN A NAME?

1. Moses: See Exodus 2:1-10
2. Uittenbogaard, Arie. "The Amazing Name Moses: Meaning and Etymology." Abarim Publications. Accessed June 03, 2019. http://www.abarim-publications.com/Meaning/Moses.html#.XPRxrVNKjOQ.
3. Jacob See Genesis 28
4. Campbell, Mike. "Meaning / History Comments for the Name Jaden." Behind the Name. Accessed June 03, 2019. https://www.behindthename.com/name/jaden/comments/history. (pg 35).

CHAPTER 5. OPENNESS IN ADOPTION

1. "April Dinwoodie Remarks on Adoption." C. Accessed June 03, 2019. https://www.c-span.org/video/?417825-1/april-dinwoodie-remarks-adoption.
2. "April Dinwoodie." April Dinwoodie. Accessed January 03, 2019. https://aprildinwoodie.com/.

CHAPTER 7. NOT UNICORNS

1. Barnett, Alex, Multiracial Family Man Podcast (March 4, 2018) https://multiracialfamilyman.libsyn.com/size/5/?search=LIGIA

CHAPTER 8. CELEBRATE ADOPTION

1. Moline, Karen. "Trading "Gotcha Day" for "Adoption Day"." Adoptive Families. July 15, 2016. Accessed January 13, 2019. (pg.47-48) https://www.adoptivefamilies.com/adoption-bonding-home/gotcha-day-placement/.
2. Riben, Mirah, and Mirah Riben. "The Insensitivity of Adoption Day Celebrations." HuffPost. December 07, 2017. Accessed March 03, 2019. https://www.huffpost.com/entry/the-insensitivity-of-adoption-day-celebrations_n_7207100. (pg 50)

CHAPTER 9. ADOPTION AND THE CLASSROOM

1. MZill, N., & Wilcox, W. B. (2018, March 26). The Adoptive Difference: New Evidence on How Adopted Children Perform in School. Retrieved

June 21, 2019, from https://ifstudies.org/blog/the-adoptive-difference-new-evidence-on-how-adopted-children-perform-in-school.

CHAPTER 11. LOVE IS NOT ALL YOU NEED

1. Cain, Barbara S., MSW. "Double-Dip Feelings: Stories to Help Children Understand Emotions." American Psychological Association. Accessed June 03, 2019. https://www.apa.org/pubs/magination/4418110.
2. Barnett, Alex. "Afro-Latina Culture, Multiracial Life in the South, and Transracial Adoption, with Ligia Cushman, Ep. 158." Multiracial Media. March 04, 2018. Accessed June 03, 2019. http://multiracialmedia.com/afro-latina-culture-multiracial-life-in-the-south-and-transracial-adoption-with-ligia-cushman-ep-158/.

CHAPTER 12. HEARD

1. Johnson, Jason. "The Echoes of Christmas in Adoption." BLOG. December 17, 2015. Accessed June 03, 2019. http://jasonjohnsonblog.com/blog/the-echo-christmas-in-adoption.
2. Perez, Rich. Mi Casa Uptown: Learning to Love Again. Nashville, TN: B & H Publishing Group, 2017.

Made in the USA
Monee, IL
30 September 2021

79102700R00049